My Balloon Ride

Gare Thompson

Contents

Introduction

The Perfect Day!

My alarm goes off. It is very early in the morning. I look out my window. It is barely light. It looks like a perfect day to go hot-air ballooning. I dress quickly and go outside. The air is cool and still. There are no strong winds. Yes, it is the right kind of weather to go ballooning. Dad, my sister, and I put our equipment in the truck. We are off!

We are going to a hot-air balloon **rally**. There will be more than 100 balloons in the air! There will be balloons of different shapes and colors. I cannot wait to get there.

People inflate hot-air balloons at a rally.

Chapter 1

Getting Ready

We arrive at the rally. The air is still cool. We drive into the large flat field to unload. Two of my Dad's friends join us. They are experienced **balloonists**. I am glad that they are here. Dad tells me it is time to work.

First, we take out the wicker **basket**. The basket is what we will ride in. It contains instruments that help the balloon fly safely. We set the basket on its side.

Next, we set up the **envelope**. The envelope, which looks like a big balloon, is what holds the air. The envelope is made of very strong nylon. It is very heavy. We spread out the envelope. Then we attach the envelope to the basket with **cables**.

Finally, we fasten a burner to the top of the basket. We will use the burner to heat the air inside the envelope. The heated air is what lifts the balloon off the ground.

▼ **Balloonists spread out the envelope of their balloon on the ground.**

▲ **Balloonists hold open the mouth of their balloon as they inflate it.**

Dad says that the equipment is all set. Now we are ready to **inflate**, or fill, the balloon with air. Dad's friends hold open the mouth of the balloon. The mouth is the huge opening at the bottom of the balloon. Then, Dad sets a fan next to the basket. It blows air into the envelope.

I hold a rope that is attached to the top of the balloon. The rope keeps the balloon from rolling from side to side as it fills with air. It also keeps the envelope in line with the basket. Dad tells me to hold it steady. The balloon begins to take a round shape as it fills with air.

Soon, the balloon is almost filled with air. However, the air in the balloon must be heated. Otherwise, the balloon will not rise. Dad turns on the burner. A flame, taller than my dad, shoots out. It heats the air inside the balloon.

Dad keeps the burner going until the envelope begins to lift off the ground. The balloon slowly rises. I have to make sure the balloon doesn't rise too fast. It seems like it takes a long time. But it only takes about five minutes to inflate the balloon. The balloon is soon standing tall. It is almost as tall as a seven-story building.

▼ **The burner on the top of the basket produces a large flame that heats the air inside the balloon.**

▼ **A balloon lays on its side until the air that is inside it is heated.**

Dad wants to check the wind one more time. He fills a small red balloon with gas. He lets the balloon go. The balloon shows the wind's direction and speed. Dad says the winds are blowing a little over two miles (3 kilometers) per hour. This is good. If the winds had been blowing at eight miles (13 kilometers) per hour or more, it would have been too dangerous to fly.

Two of Dad's friends hold down the basket as we climb in. The basket holds four passengers, but today there are only three of us. Before they let go of the basket, Dad gives the burner one more blast. The air must be hot enough to carry our weight. Now it is hot enough to carry us up, up, and away!

All around us the other balloons are ready, too. Some balloons have already lifted off. I watch them float up. I look up into the balloon. It is amazing to see the balloon full. Dad gives his friends a signal. It is our turn. The men slowly let go of the basket. Dad checks his instruments. We are off!

We give the balloon another blast from the burner as we prepare to take off. ▶

Chapter 2

Flying Along

The lift-off feels smooth. It feels like someone is slowly pulling us into the air by a string. We travel at the same speed as the wind, so we don't feel or hear it. Dad stays by the burner. He needs to blast the burner if the air in the envelope gets cool. The air has to stay hot to keep us flying.

We rise high in the sky. We are almost a mile (1 1/2 kilometers) high. Dad checks the wind and its direction. Then he lets the balloon go down about 300 feet (80 meters). Now, we will fly at this **altitude**, or height. Dad tells us to look out and enjoy the view.

Dad blasts the burner every two or three minutes. If he wants us to go up higher, he blasts the burner for a longer time. The hotter the air in the envelope, the higher we go. Dad lets the air in the envelope cool to fly lower.

There is nothing between the ground and us. But I am not afraid. I feel safe in the balloon. Our trip will last about an hour. Dad is not sure how far we will go. The distance covered depends on how fast the wind is blowing. Dad says the wind is blowing at a pretty fast speed.

We are not as far up as an airplane, but we are up higher than the treetops. I look below us. This must be what things look like to a bird. Everything is so small. Cows look more like cats. The balloon starts to lower. We float down toward the treetops.

I ask Dad if we can follow the road below. It curves around trees and goes through a small town. Dad says he can't follow the road. Steering a balloon is not like steering a car or a bike. Balloons fly where the wind takes them. Dad says that is why ballooning is such an adventure.

We keep going at a nice steady pace. There are some horses beneath us. They are quietly munching on grass. Dad blasts the burner. He wants us to go higher so we don't disturb them.

Dad contacts our **crew** on a two-way radio. They will help us land the balloon. Since we don't know where we will end up, they have to follow us in the truck. We tell them what we can see and where we think we are.

It is hard to be in the crew trying to follow a balloon. Sometimes, the roads we spot are closed. Other times, the crew is not sure what **landmark** we are describing. Dad told them about a large field of wheat that we were passing. But that did not help. There are many fields of wheat in this area. Finally, Dad sees a large odd-shaped rock. He tells the crew what it looks like. Now, they know what road we are above. The crew does a good job of tracking us.

The fuel is running low. It is time to land. Dad cannot turn the balloon around and go back to the take-off spot. He looks for a large, flat space to land the balloon. It does not seem as though we have been up here for almost an hour, but we have. I'd like to stay up here forever. Dad laughs. He reminds me that hot-air balloons cannot fly at night. They do not have lights like planes.

We spot a large, open space. It is a field where horses and cows graze. There are no animals there now. Dad radios the crew. He asks them to get permission for us to land there. The crew finds the farmhouse. The farmer says we can land in his field. Dad lets the air in the envelope cool. Without the burner blasting, it is very quiet in the balloon. Slowly, the balloon begins to drop down.

Chapter 3

Landing

Landing is tricky. Dad must time the burner just right. We cannot go down too fast or too slow. If we do, we could miss the **landing site**. Dad checks the area. He makes sure that there are no power lines or other tall structures we could hit.

Dad also tries to avoid trees. He doesn't want the branches to poke holes in the envelope. Dad prepares to land. As we get close to the ground, Dad pulls a cord to open the **vent**, a hole at the top of the envelope. This lets hot air escape slowly. The envelope begins to **deflate**. Now we can land.

The day is still calm. We will have a good landing. We slowly reach the ground. Dad says that we are lucky there was no strong wind. Otherwise, it would have been very bumpy. We touch the ground.

After a balloon lands, the envelope needs to be deflated. ▶

The crew is waiting for us. We tie down the basket. We all work quickly to deflate the balloon. We squeeze the air out of it. I like this part. Finally, the envelope is flat. We fold it and put it in its bag. We put the basket and other equipment in the crew's truck. Dad pops open a bottle of sparkling cider. We toast one another. It has been a good ride. I can't wait to do it again!

Epilogue

Festivals and Fun

Dad is going to take me to the biggest balloon festival in the world. It is held every year in Albuquerque, New Mexico. Hundreds of hot-air balloons will be flying there. Many of the balloons are different shapes. Some look like animals. It will be a magical sight to see all the balloons in the sky.

Balloonists often play games at festivals. One game is called "Fox and Hounds." The balloon called the "fox" takes off first. Later, other balloons called the "hounds" take off. The hound that lands closest to the fox wins.

Another game uses special beanbags. One balloon flies off and lands in a large, flat field. The crew makes a huge X in the field. The X can be seen from the air. Then other balloonists follow the path of the first balloon. They drop their beanbags as near to the center of the X as they can. It's hard to do because the winds change. This makes it difficult to drop the beanbag close to the X!

Next year I turn ten. Dad says that we can go somewhere special to fly our balloon. But I think I'll ask him to fly over our town. I'll take my friends for a ride. It will be fun to see our town from the balloon. We can fly over the river and the fields. I wonder what our town will look like from the air. A hot-air balloon ride will make a birthday I'll never forget!

Glossary

altitude	the height of an object in the sky
balloonists	people who fly hot-air balloons
basket	a light, sturdy container made of wicker for people to ride in
cables	strong ropes
crew	the people who help launch and land a hot-air balloon
deflate	to let air out
envelope	the part of a hot-air balloon that is inflated
inflate	to fill with air
landing site	the place where a balloon lands
landmark	a part of the landscape that stands out or is distinct
rally	a big meeting of people who like doing the same thing
vent	a hole in the top of the envelope that lets air escape from inside the balloon

Index